HOW STUDENTS SAVE OVER $10,000 A YEAR.

Effective Ways to Spend Less Money While going to School.

Emo Ikede MBA, B.Sc.

ISBN: 978-0-9948803-1-4

Cover design: Brenda_art177

Editing: Joy Ikede, Lora Archer, Basil Ikede.

Disclaimer:

Although the author has made every effort to ensure that the information in this book was correct at press time, the author does not assume and hereby disclaim any liability to any party for any loss, damage, or disruption caused by errors or omissions, whether such errors or omissions result from negligence, accident, or any other cause.

Table of Contents

INTRODUCTION

I have seen many College and University graduates struggle to move ahead financially because they are burdened by debt they accumulated during their student years. I feel many of them would have had less debt if they had the right information to help them make better financial decisions. When one realizes that most of us start building our credit history immediately after high school, it becomes increasingly important to make financial education a priority even before we start University or College.

Every day, students make decisions that affect their financial well-being. Examples include deciding on where to buy textbooks, what and where to eat, mode of transportation, courses to take, accommodation etc. Sometimes students make these decisions without fully understanding how it may affect their financial well-being in the future.

To address this, I wrote this book to provide students with information that would help them look at their income and expense, compare options, and then make choices that would save the most money. Costs like tuition are fixed, however there are many other areas where students can make smart choices that cost less, and still get good value for their money.

This book gives student the awareness, tool and focus, for making the right decisions that would ultimately help in saving money during their time of studies, and in the future, after they graduate.

Target Audience

Students, Parents, Counsellors, and Student Advisors.

Book Layout

The format is simple. I show you how to look at your top expense areas and suggest ways to reduce costs in each one. The steps are easy to follow and only require your decision and dedication to accomplish.

Estimated annual savings are shown in brackets at the beginning of some sections.

How to Use it

1. Quickly read through to get an idea of the areas you can save money.
2. Create your budget so you are clear on your cash flow (money coming in and going out).
3. Tackle each budget area to find areas you can reduce costs. Use the suggestions in the book as your guide.

Note

Since the cost of living varies depending on where you live, your calculations may be a bit higher or lower than the estimates in this book. The principles and strategies presented will still work everywhere.

BUDGETING

Why You Should Create a Budget

A budget gives you a clear picture of your total income and expense. It helps you track your spending and reveals areas you can save money. It is easier to take control of your money when you have a record of where you spend it and exactly how much you spend on each transaction. A budget quickly shows if you spend more or less than your income.

Also, having a budget makes it easier for you to follow the recommendations in this book and calculate how much you can save when you make changes to your spending habits.

From your budget, you can spot areas to cut back and save money when you prioritize between your needs and wants.

How to Create a Budget

Advances in computer and smart phone technology make it easier than ever to create a budget. You can use a template, program or phone app (free or paid) that is readily available online. Depending on your phone or computer operating system, you can search online for websites that allow you to create customizable budgets, free Microsoft Excel templates or even download budget apps for your cell phone or tablet (Google Play, Apple App Store) that make it easy for you to track your spending habits.

Many universities and colleges have a free estimating tool on their website that you can use to get a sense of how much it would cost you each year to attend their institution. Options you can select include living on or off campus, meal plans, health and dental plan, program of study, books and supplies, fun, miscellaneous etc. The options you select increase or decrease your total cost estimate.

Your goal should be to try a few budget tools till you find one that you like, and find easy to use. Features of a good budget tool include: multiple income and expense categories, easy editing, automatic calculation of totals, portability, easy access etc.

You can also try the "**Budget Tool**" on my website (**www.ejitech.com/howtosavemoney/tools**).

Budget Tips

1. Remember to include all sources of income and expense.
2. Have separate entries for your top expenses.
3. Lump similar expenses into one. For example, buying coffee and lunches can be grouped into an expense category called "eating out".
4. Record expenses frequently and close to when you make them. This way, you don't forget them, and you are not overwhelmed by trying to enter a month or more worth of expenses at once.
5. Look for areas where you spent more than you expected or where you can reduce costs.
6. Refer back to your budget when reading through this book to address expense areas that are good candidates for reducing costs.

ACCOMMODATION

($8000 or more annual savings)

Accommodation Choices

As a student, you have 4 choices for accommodation: Stay at Home, Single Apartment, Shared Apartment or Campus Residence. Your cost for each choice varies, with staying at home being your least expensive option (pretty much free).

Stay at Home

A strong argument can be made for picking a school close to your parents' home if it offers the program you want to take. By staying at home, you save on rent (which can run you anywhere between $6,000 and $15,000 a year based on location). You also get the bonus of free food and laundry which saves you an additional $3,600 - $5,000 per year.

It is not always possible for a student to stay at home (program not offered close to home, or issues at home etc.), so the pros and cons of the other 3 accommodation choices are discussed below.

Single Apartment

Renting a single apartment (alone) tends to be one of the more expensive options because you are responsible for 100% of the costs. You should pay attention to what is included and excluded in your rent. The cost of utilities such as heat, hot water, electricity and air-conditioning will increase your monthly expenses especially if you live in an area that has very cold and long winters or is very hot. If utilities are not included and you are still interested in the apartment, you can ask your landlord or the Power (Electric) and Water Company for a cost history print-out, so that you can make a more informed decision.

Advantages to renting a single apartment include: no roommate compatibility issues, privacy for studying, control over noise levels etc.

Shared Apartment

Shared apartment gives the renters 50% or more savings when compared to the single apartment option. The more people in a shared apartment, the greater the savings. For example 4 people sharing a 4 bedroom apartment tend to pay less than 2 people sharing a 2 bedroom apartment in the same neighbourhood. Savings extend to shared internet, TV and even food costs.

Disadvantages include: potential for roommate compatibility issues (noisy, messy, eating your food)

Campus Residence

Most large Universities and Colleges have residential facilities on or close to the campus. They tend to offer optional meal plans that students can purchase, and rent includes heat, hot-water, electricity and internet access.

Advantages include: Location. By being on or near campus, the student does not need a car and is only a few minutes walking distance from classes. The meal plan (even though on the expensive side) helps students manage their food budget, and saves them time from buying and preparing meals.

Disadvantages include: Price (tend to be more expensive than renting shared accommodation), rooms may not include a kitchen, so you cannot prepare meals, residence can be noisy and distracting and washroom facilities are shared.

Suggestions

1. Start with your budget to see how much money you have for accommodation. Use this as a guide to determine what you can afford.
2. Remember to include transportation cost and commute times when comparing apartments.
3. In shared accommodation arrangements, make sure all roommates sign the lease so that everyone bears equal responsibility for expenses.
4. It is a good idea to consider roommate compatibility when deciding with whom to share accommodations.
5. When sharing cost on things like food, decide on what items make sense to buy in bulk (fruit, eggs, milk etc.)

6. Agree to try cost sharing for a month or two and if it works out well, continue, if not, stop.

TUITION

Fixed

Tuition is one of the biggest expenses you face as a student. Unfortunately, it is a non-negotiable amount that is set by each school and varies based on the courses you take.

Although different schools have different tuition prices for the same program, when trying to decide between schools, you should include other expenses and factors (accommodation, transportation, quality and reputation of the school etc.) to help you make a more informed decision. Most of this information can be found on the schools website and 3rd party publications (print or online) that compare and rank schools.

Suggestions

1. Remember to include tuition in your budget.
2. When comparing schools, remember that tuition is only one of many factors needed for a more accurate picture of the true cost of attending each school. So, make sure you include reputation of the School, accommodation, facilities, amenities etc. to enable you get a clearer picture of the school that is best for you.
3. If you have prior learning related to your course of study, check to see if you are eligible for course exemptions. Since most schools charge tuition by the

course, an exemption means you do not take or pay for the course, which means you save money.

Projected Market Demand and Expected Salary

When making decisions about what to study, take time to research current and projected labour market demand and expected salary for each field of study.

There is the argument that you should only study what you are passionate about because when you do, the money will follow. I agree with choosing a field of study based on passion, however I still think it is important that you find out about the market demand and expected salary so at least you know what to expect when you graduate. This helps you make an informed return on investment assessment of your education choice.

You can find more information on labour market demand and salary by searching online, and also by talking to a career counselor at your school.

FOOD

($3000 or more annual savings)

Food costs is usually the next large expense a student has to deal with, after accommodation and tuition. Here are a few suggestions that would help reduce costs.

Groceries

1. Buy in bulk but only purchase what you can finish before the product goes bad or expires. Spoiled food that you throw out negates savings gained from bulk purchases.
2. Buy generic or store-brand products instead of brand-name ones. This can save you 30% or more.
3. To make sure you are getting a similar product, compare the ingredients between the generic and brand-name item. If similar, buy the cheaper generic one and try it out to see if it passes your taste and quality test. If it does, then you've found a bargain.
4. Use sales flyers to plan your shopping trip and advantage of discounts.
5. Stick to a budget.
6. Use coupons if you have them. They save you a lot of money over time.
7. Keep in mind that most grocery stores have sales on regular items like meat and fish on a 2 to 5 week cycle. This means that as long as you have a freezer, you can buy enough on sale to last you for at least 3 weeks, and then buy again when the next sale cycle comes up. This

way, you always end up paying less than the regular prices (savings of 20% to 50%).

8. Try not to shop when you are hungry. When hungry, you tend to make more impulse purchases, thus buying more than you need.

9. Compare Unit Price to find the cheaper product. Most stores post the unit price of each item underneath the purchase price. You can use the unit price to compare brands and sizes, as they are all priced against the same measurement (for example, per 100ml). The cheapest product is the one with the lowest unit price

Meals

Prepare your meals instead of buying ready-made, packaged or frozen meals. You end up reducing the cost of your meals by 50% or more. This is not to completely ignore packaged meals or eating out. You could do this when in a bind or as a treat for yourself once in a while.

Vending Machine

Products in vending machines are usually priced three times as much as the store price. If you buy the item on a regular basis, you are better off going to the store. An example is sport drinks. The vending machine price for a bottle is $3, where as you can buy a 24 pack for $12 at the store (unit price of $0.50). In this example, the vending machine price is 6 times as much as the store price.

Coffee & Tea

Depending on where you shop, you pay between $1.50 and $5.00 for a hot beverage. However if you make it at home or in your lunch room, it costs you less than $0.10 a cup, depending on whether or not you add milk and sugar. If you have a cup a day and make it yourself, it would only cost you $37 for the year. However if you buy it from a coffee shop, it would cost you between $548 and $1825 for the year.

Bottled Water

If your school has filtered water fountains, you can save on the cost of buying bottled water by filling up your cup or container from the water fountain. Doing this saves you about $3 a day, which works out to about $1095 a year.

Sandwich

It doesn't take much effort or time to make a sandwich or wrap, and it only costs a fraction of what it costs to buy it ready-made. Make sure you plan ahead by including ingredients for it on your grocery list.

Fruit

Buy a bunch of bananas or a bag of apples instead of a single fruit. This helps you significantly reduce the price you pay per fruit. If you have roommates, you can split the cost and share the fruit to reduce the chance of it going bad before it is all eaten up.

FUN

"All work and no play make you cranky and grumpy. So does over-spending on fun".

Making time and saving money for fun help relives stress, take your mind off school work for a moment and energize you to face another day.

Budget for "Fun"

Remember the budget I got you to create earlier on in this book? Yes that one. I hope you included allocating money for "fun" in it. The key is to stick to the amount you budgeted, which means if you spend all your "fun" money for the month on the first weekend of the month, then you have to be disciplined enough to wait till the next month before you dip into your "fun" budget again. (Do-able but sometimes easier said than done especially when your friends are pressuring you to go for a night out).

When you spend more than your allocated "fun" budget, you end up dipping into funds you had allocated for something else. This is a good way to undermine your budget and make it less effective in the long run.

Suggestions

1. Review your budget and make sure you allocate a realistic amount for "fun".

2. To make it easier to manage, you can divide your "fun budget" amount by 4 to get how much you can spend each week.
3. If you go overboard (yes it happens to all of us at one time or another), don't be too hard on yourself. Try to get on track the next month. Just don't use it as an excuse to get you off your budget all the time.
4. Accept that sometimes, unforeseen circumstances cause us to spend more than budgeted. (e.g. you accidentally damage your compute beyond repair and need to get a new one)
5. Sticking to your budget teaches and enforces discipline. Learning this now will save you a lot of money and headaches down the road.
6. Make sure your "fun budget" does not take money away from top priorities such as tuition, food, accommodation, transportation and books. Always prioritize so that you always have money for the important things.

TRANSPORTATION

($4000 or more annual savings)

Car

Having a car while going to school is cool and convenient, but it comes at a price. Some students are fortunate enough to afford one (savings, good job, wealthy parents) while it is a stretch for others. Remember, you are in school to get a great education and good grades. The balance is to make sure your car does not detract you from that goal.

If you have a part-time job to pay for your car, and you struggle to find enough time to study, it might be time to decide if keeping the car is in your best interest.

Depending on the city you're in and the distance from your residence to school, you have other transportation options that can save you money. They include public transit, car-pooling, biking or walking.

Ongoing Car Costs

The cost of owning a car goes beyond the original purchase price, lease or monthly payments. When you include the cost of insurance, maintenance, repairs, tires, registration, parking etc. you can easily spend up to $6,000 or more each year for the privilege of owning a car.

Car Pooling

You can advertise online (classified or social network) that you are looking for someone with whom to carpool each day. You simply state the time of day, pickup point and destination. If you own a car, the payments you receive from the person carpooling with you will help offset your transportation costs. If you don't own a car, you might be able to negotiate a carpool price that is less than public transportation.

Be aware of some of the drawbacks of carpooling which include: flexibility (the day that one of you has to leave before or after your regularly scheduled time) and also the initial process of arranging transportation with a stranger. To mitigate the flexibility issue, you should include cost reductions for such days in your carpooling agreement.

Public Transit

Many cities offer bus/transit passes to students at a substantial discount. Depending on your city, and with your student discount, you can buy an annual transit pass for less than $700.

Let's Do the Math

Over the course of a 4 year degree program:

Owning a car = $24,000

Using Public Transit = $2,800

Money Saved with public transit = $21,200

Food for Thought

- What would you do with an additional $21,200 at the end of a 4 year degree?
- Will it help towards paying down your student loan?
- Can you use it towards a down payment for a house when you start working?
- Will it cover the costs of nice vacation after you graduate?
- A cheap used car will still cost you over $3,000 a year for maintenance, gas and insurance.

Car Insurance

If you own a car, here are a couple of things you can do to make sure you get the insurance coverage you need at the lowest price.

1. Check to see if you qualify for a multi-policy (household) discount if you get your car insurance with the same company as your parents.
2. Request multiple quotes from different companies.
3. Ask your Student Affairs office if any companies offer discounts to students enrolled in your institution.
4. Raise your deductible limit to a higher amount you are comfortable with. This will reduce your annual premium.
5. Consider getting only the basic (lowest) insurance coverage on an older vehicle especially if the value of the car is less than $3500.

6. Every 2 years, request quotes from multiple insurance companies to make sure you are still getting the best price.

COMMUNICATION

($400 or more annual savings)

Cell Phone

Cell phone plans and prices vary from region to region, for example, when you compare Canada, USA and the UK. This means the amount of savings you can achieve by implementing suggestions below will also vary depending on where you live.

However a few common strategies can help you reduce your cell phone bill. They include:

1. Don't buy the data plan if you have free Wi-Fi at school and at home.
2. Get a plan with unlimited text since texts are cheaper than phone calls.
3. Look for promotions and sales geared towards students (ask if student discounts are offered).
4. Shop around (online) for the best deals and plans based on your usage patterns.
5. Get a low-end to mid-range phone that suits your intended use.
6. See if the pay-as-you-go plans meet your need (Note that although their base monthly cost is less expensive than contract plans, their talk (minute) rate is usually higher).

Home Phone

1. If you already have a cell phone, consider cancelling your home phone.
2. If you must have a home phone, make sure you don't take on extra features if not included in the basic price (call minder, voice mail, etc.)
3. Don't pay for voice mail. You can easily buy an answering machine for a one-time fee that is usually less than the annual cost for the voice mail feature.
4. Shop around. Check a few providers to see who has the best deal.
5. Consider VoIP which tends to cost less than the standard phone service.

VoIP (free calls & discounted long-distance calling)

Quite a number of companies let you make free VoIP calls from your computer, tablet or smart-phone to landlines. Google Gmail for example offers free VoIP calls to anywhere in North America (as of the time of writing). Also a search at the App store of your smart device or phone will give you choices of Apps that let you make free device to landline phone calls.

Don't forget good old staples like Facebook, Skype, FaceTime or WhatsApp that let you communicate (voice, video messages etc.) for free. Search and find what works best for you.

There are companies that offer significantly reduced long distance plans via VoIP. You reward for doing your research is that you will keep in touch with friends and family for free or next to nothing.

BOOKS

($500 or more annual savings)

New Textbooks

New textbooks are expensive, and depending on the structure of your course, you may need a copy on hand to complete required readings and assignments. Each textbook generally cost between $50 to $300, so a full time student can easily spend up to $1000 or more per semester just on books. To reduce costs, you can split the cost of a book with a classmate. However this may not be practical at all times especially when you both need the book at the same time to complete an assignment, or when preparing ahead for class or exams. There may be times where you have no other choice but to buy new textbooks. Doing a comparative search online may help you get a discount on your purchase.

Below are a few options to reduce how much you spend on textbooks.

Rent Textbooks Online

You can rent textbooks for 2 to 6 months at a fraction of the cost of buying a new copy. Usually these are electronic copies that you access via the internet and come with useful features such as portability, search, electronic bookmarking, and highlighting etc. Examples of such websites include "Coursesmart.com" and "Chegg.com". Do an online search to find out what is available and compare prices to snag discounts.

Used Textbooks

Used textbooks tend to cost between 30% - 80% less than new ones. The challenge is finding them and getting them delivered to you on time. A good way to get a head start in hunting for used textbooks is to get your book requirements from your school as early as possible and start looking before everyone does.

You can find used books on the websites of popular books stores such as Amazon or BookScouter. However you can get better discounts when you buy them from students that just completed the course or from online classified websites. Local is safer because, you can look over the book before you purchase.

You can post "wanted" ads on social media school groups, check Faculty bulletin boards, or ask students taking the class ahead of you if you can buy their books when they are done. Just make sure you check your curriculum to ascertain the textbook is still valid for the course, before you buy.

Borrow from the Library (School or Public)

Sometimes the School or Public library carries a copy of the textbook you need for your course, if you find one to borrow, it cost you nothing so it is worth checking. The strategy here is to check the library's inventory (most are now online) before the Semester starts, and also check how many times you can renew borrowing before you have to finally return it to inventory.

Free Online Public Domain Books

Some publishers make versions of their textbooks available for free as online public domain books. You can do a search on "Google books", your school library network, or online to see if a version of your required textbook is available. Sometimes you might only find an older edition of the textbook. You can then ask your teacher if it's okay to use it instead of the newer edition.

Older Editions of Textbook

You can buy or get older editions of textbooks from the library, classified websites, former students or online book retailers. These copies sell for much less than the new editions. Again you should first check with your teacher to make sure you can use them.

Sell your Textbooks

Consider selling your textbooks after you are done with them. You can expect to get back 30% - 80% of what you paid for the books, depending on the edition and physical condition of the book. Avenues to sell your textbooks include classified websites, your Department's bulletin board and social media page, online book retailers (Amazon, BookScouter & EBay etc.).

Bottom Line

If you take the time to buy textbooks based on the examples above, you are more likely to reduce how much you pay for some of your textbooks, which in turn reduces your overall expense.

Remember to start early and take time to check as many options as possible.

ENTERTAINMENT

($350 or more annual savings)

TV

Many of us love watching TV. The cable and satellite TV providers offer hundreds of channels to us for a price. Questions you should ask yourself before deciding on a TV package include:

1. How much TV will I really be watching?
2. Do I need to have TV service or can I cut the cord and get all my news and entertainment directly from the internet?
3. If I plan to get TV service, are there companies that offer package discounts for TV, Internet, and Phone that I can take advantage of?

Internet

Buy a package that suits your use. If all you use your internet for is email, web surfing and watching movies, you don't need the highest, fastest or most expensive package.

Movies & Music

Remember that websites like YouTube give you access to free music 24/7 and many TV stations provide free website access to popular programs 1 day after they are broadcast on live TV.

Also websites like NETFLIX provide huge libraries of movies for a low monthly fee while others like CRACKLE offer free content.

The bottom line is you have options for all your entertainment and information needs that range from free or low cost to paid subscription. When trying to save money, free makes for a pretty good deal. Remember to search and ask for student discounts because every dollar saved helps you spend less.

EMPLOYMENT

($3000 - $20,000 income)

Some students work part-time to help cover their expenses. In today's 24/7 business environment, coupled with technology advancements, it easier to tele-work or run an online business. As a result, an increasing number of students look to part-time employment to help pay for their college education.

Pros

1. You start building experience on your resume.
2. You earn money.
3. You pick-up work-life skills.

Cons

1. Takes away time from studying.
2. Reduces available downtime.
3. Increases stress from balancing work and school commitments.

It is a good idea to look for work with flexible hours so that you can scale down or ramp up your work hours depending on your school workload and calendar. An example is working less hours during Mid-term and Final exams.

The key is to make sure your part-time work does not adversely affect your school work and grades.

When applying, make sure you submit a professional looking resume to improve your chance of getting the job. You can find samples online or at the students and community employment center.

Where to Find Work

1. Campus websites and bulletin boards.
2. New media companies that allow tele-working (Web, Freelance, Graphic Designer, Blogger, Answering Service, Tech-Support etc.)
3. Local businesses, especially ones that are open 12 to 24 hours a day that would easily accommodate your schedule.
4. Student employment center (on or off campus).
5. Recruiting companies. (Be prepared to create a profile and post your resume).
6. Job & Employment websites.
7. Social media. For example posting the position you seek on LinkedIn.

BANKING

($200 or more annual savings)

No Fee Bank Account

You can save a few dollars a month by reducing or even totally eliminating banking fees. Many banks offer no-fee banking to students. You get free chequing, free debit card swiping and free online banking. This way you save when you write cheques and also save the 30 – 60 cents fee per debit card swipe transaction that the other banks charge when you go over a fixed number of deposits per month.

The amounts saved each month might seem small, but over a period of time, it would add up to a significant amount that will help you on your path to financial freedom. Every dollar saved counts.

It is worth mentioning that some of the smaller banks give interest rate on your savings that is more than what the big banks offer. Look at this as one of the things to check off when choosing a bank.

Banking Dos

1. Search for banks that offer free banking to students.
2. Use ATM's on the bank's network to avoid transaction fees.
3. Make sure you read and understand the terms of your bank account so that you avoid surprise charges.

4. Find out what interest rate the bank charges on loans, or gives on account balances.

*** Warning on Instant Loan Companies (avoid them)!!!

Most cities and towns have companies (not banks) that provide short term loans. Some advertise that you can get instant cash by just showing them your pay stub (proof of income). The offer sounds good when you are cash strapped and looking for a quick fix, but the caveat is that they charge outrageous interest rates that on an annual basis can be over 170% (yikes!!)

To show you how dangerous a 170% annual charge is, if you borrowed $5000 and did not make any payments, after 5 months you will owe over $10,000 and after 10 months, $20,000. In short, the money owed doubles every 5 months. Now that is super scary.

Suggestion: If you need a short term loan, you are better off going to the bank or getting it from family. Compared to getting one of those instant loans, you are still better off using your credit card even at the rate of 19%.

CREDIT CARDS

They are Not Free

The main free feature on some credit cards is the "no-annual fee" clause. Credit cards should be called "**debt**" cards, because any balance you do not pay in full past the grace period (approximate 21 days) becomes a high interest loan. Interest rate for first time card holders can be as high as 19% or more per annum, depending on their credit history.

High credit card interest rates affect you the most when you only make the minimum payment. This makes your balance grow faster than your payments can reduce the principal. In the scenario below, you end up paying more in interest than the initial amount you charged on the card.

For example if you start out with a $5000 balance and only make the 2% minimum payment ($100) each month, you end up paying a total of $10,830 at the end ($5000 principal at 19.99% interest over a 9 years and 1 month payback period). Why would you want to carry a balance for 9 years? (See table below).

If on the other hand you pay $200 each month instead of the minimum payment, you end up paying your debt in 2 years and 9 months with a total of $6521. That is a $4309 savings in interest when compared to only paying the minimum.

The best case scenario is you plan ahead and save for your purchase so that you can pay in full. The benefit is that you do not pay any interest.

Balance	$ 5000	$ 5000	$ 5000
Interest Charged	19.99 %	19.99 %	19.99%
Monthly Payment (%)	2 %	4 %	100%
Monthly Payment ($)	$ 100	$ 200	$5,000
Payback Period	9 years and 1 month	2 years and 9 months	immediate
Total cost (interest included)	$10,830	$ 6,521	$5,000
Savings	$ 0	$ 4,309	$5,830

Suggestions

1. Shop around for the lowest rate.
2. Only purchase what you can pay back at the due date.
3. Ask for a $500 or $1,000 credit limit to reduce your liability.
4. Only get one credit card (easier to manage).
5. Always try to pay more than the minimum payment. The more you pay the better.
6. Don't get cash advances on your credit card. If you do, you immediately get charged interest on the money withdrawn at a rate higher than the base credit card rate.

Credit Card Exclusive Transactions

If you are scared of going overboard with credit cards, but still need one for transactions that can only be made by credit card, you can search for banks that offer "debit credit cards". A debit credit card is one where your credit limit is equal to the amount of money you deposit into your credit card account. The advantage is that you get all the functionality of a regular credit card with the added bonus of only being able to spend money that you have. This makes it impossible for you go into debt.

You can use the debit credit card for transactions such as online purchases, car rentals, airline tickets and hotel bookings, just as you would with a regular credit card.

STUDENT DISCOUNTS

(10% - 25%)

Discounts are Free Money

In many University and College towns, some businesses offer discounts to students with a valid students ID card. Businesses and services discounted include transportation, food, retail and entertainment. For some, you have to buy a discount card, while others give a flat percentage discount on items purchased.

While doing my MBA, I bought groceries on Tuesdays because the 2 main groceries stores in my city offered a 10% discount to students on everything purchased, as long as they showed their valid ID. I shopped this way for my household and saved over $550 each year I was in school.

I am surprised to see that many students do not take advantage of this, even though the stores clearly advertise it.

Finding Discounts

Here are some places to find businesses offering student discounts:

1. Campus bulletin boards.
2. Fellow students.
3. Social media.
4. Directly from businesses. You might be pleasantly surprised.

5. Flyers and advertisements.
6. Department of Students Services on campus.
7. Local web search.

Suggestions

1. Take time to search for discounts and keep an ear and eye out for them.
2. Plan shopping (time and store) to take advantage of discounts offered.
3. Use social media to ask classmates and senior students about discount opportunities.

SHOPPING

($400 or more annual savings)

Clothes

Some of the best savings for clothing happen at the end of each season. For example heavily discounted winter clothing can be bought at the end of February or March, which also coincides with the after-Christmas-slow-down experienced in retail stores. At this time, stores tend to offer significant discount on their merchandise in order to clear the store for the upcoming season.

The ultimate savings on clothes comes from used clothing stores. For example, you can buy a pair of jeans at a used store for only $8 as opposed to $30 to $80 at the retail store. Also, a good winter jacket at the used clothing store costs less than $20. A similar jacket from a retail store may cost over $100.

At used clothing stores, you sometimes find clothes that still have price tags from the regular retail store where they were liquidated. These items are brand new, never been worn, but are sold at significantly reduced prices.

Furniture

You can find used furniture at classified websites or used furniture stores for a fraction of their regular retail price. Many of these used furniture items may simply need a good cleaning or sanding to make them as good as new.

Tools

A used hammer or screw driver set works as well as a new one, but costs less. You can find used tools on classified websites or discounted ones at clearance sales in regular retail stores. Don't forget you can always borrow tools from friends and family for free.

Also if you need a tool that you would use only once, you can look into renting it from stores that do so for a fraction of the purchase price.

TOTAL COST OF OWNERSHIP (TCO)

Some items we purchase have ongoing maintenance costs that add up over time. When making purchase decisions on these items, failing to consider the TCO can make you think the best deal is the item in the store with the lowest initial cost (sticker price).

Example 1

Printers are a good example for showing TCO because students need to print many pages of assignments, reports and articles while in school.

Comparing the TCO between inkjet and laser printers.

These days, you can buy a brand new inkjet printer, complete with starter ink, for less than $40. Replacement inkjet cartridges may cost about $40 each and give you a print output of 200 pages. Ongoing costs of printing a page is $0.20 ($40/200).

You can buy a desktop laser printer (monochrome with starter toner) for $60. Replacement toner cartridges may cost about $60 and give you a print output of 1500 pages. Ongoing cost of printing a page is $0.04 ($60/1500)

Note that it costs 5 times as much to print on the inkjet printer when compared to printing on the laser printer.

If we assume a student prints about 1500 pages over the course of their schooling:

TCO for the inkjet printer would be $320 ($40 purchase + $280 for 7 replacement ink cartridges).

TCO for the laser printer would be $60 ($60 purchase + no additional toner required).

By choosing the laser printer, the student would save $260 based on TCO even though the initial (store) cost of the laser printer was 50% more than the inkjet printer.

	Inkjet Printer	Laser Printer
Retail Price	$ 40	$60
Replacement cartridge	$ 40	$ 60
Output per cartridge	200 pages	1500 pages
Print cost per page	$ 0.20	$ 0.04
Cartridges for 1500 pages	8 inkjet cartridges	1 toner cartridge
Additional cartridge cost	$ 280	$ 0
TCO for 1500 pages	$ 320	$ 60
Total saved	$ 0	$ 260

Example 2

A student buys an older model used car for only $2500, but if they forget to include the TCO in their affordability calculations, they might not be prepared for the extra costs.

In a year the extra cost to own and maintain the car can be $3900 or more when you include paying for gas, insurance, repairs, registration, parking, and regular maintenance. If the student in this example has not budgeted for a total of $6400 for the car that first year, they will be in for a nasty surprise when their expenses are more than they expect.

What You Need to Know

1. Remember to include TCO calculations when deciding whether or not you can afford an item.

2. If the lowest priced item has a higher TCO, you will end up paying more for the utility (benefit) of the item when compared to one with a lower TCO.
3. Buy the item with the lowest TCO.
4. Include TCO calculations when making your budget so that you get a true picture of your expenses.

SCHOLARSHIPS

Free Money!

Many scholarships are not used because students don't apply for them. Yes it takes some time and effort to search for scholarships and complete required application forms, but when you consider it is money you don't have to pay back, it sure beats a student's loan.

Improve Your Odds

The following very likely would improve your chances of getting a scholarship.

1. Applying for every scholarship for which you qualify.
2. High academic standing in high school (good grades).
3. Going to school in your state and applying for local scholarships (Benefit of being a local resident).

Where to Find Information on Available Scholarships

1. Teachers and Guidance Counsellors at your High School.
2. Faculty staff in University or College.
3. University or College website.
4. Localized online search.

5. Past scholarship recipient list.
6. Students Affairs staff.
7. Admission staff.
8. Student's Union Executives.
9. Human Resource staff at your workplace.
10. Get your parents to check if their workplaces offer any.

STUDENT LOANS

Do You Need One?

Student loans provide funds to pay for school when you don't have enough money to cover your education costs. When you apply for a student loan, the banks assess your eligibility based on your current savings, employment prospects after you graduate based on your field of study, parents income (if you are under 25 years old) and your current job, if any.

The future job prospects assessment explains why medical, dental, engineering and pharmacy students tend to get approved easily and for a large amount of money when, compared to students in other programs with lower job prospects and income.

The time to check if you need a loan is when you start applying to schools. Use tuition and cost of living amounts information from the school's website to create your budget. If your income falls short of your expense, you should consider contacting your local bank or Credit Union to talk about applying for a student loan.

When comparing loans between creditors, look at variables like interest rate, repayment terms, transaction costs (fees for the use of debit card, writing cheques, ATM withdrawals etc.), grace period after graduation and penalty terms if you miss a payment.

Let's assume your student loan application was approved and your bank just gave you access to thousands of dollars, here are the right and wrong ways to use it.

Right Use

1. Pay for tuition.
2. Pay for books.
3. Sometimes people use it to pay for accommodation and food. I understand that sometimes that is the only option available. Don't beat up yourself for that, if you at least are not short in cash for reasons similar to the "wrong use" ones below.

Wrong Use

1. Vacation.
2. Car Purchase.
3. Partying.
4. Wardrobe update.
5. Spring break.

Remember you have to pay back the loan (with interest) when you graduate. Paying back gets difficult when you move out from home and have other living expenses to deal with. When it comes to loans, it is always a good idea to only get and use as little as needed.

HEALTH & DENTAL

Many post-secondary institutions require their students to have health insurance. Most offer a group plan that students are automatically enrolled in with fees added to tuition.

What You Need to Know

1. If you are already covered under your parent's plan or workplace plan, you can opt out of your schools plan by providing proof of existing coverage. Do this to avoid paying twice for health insurance.
2. International students can opt out by showing proof that they have private coverage (expensive out of pocket) or that their country (government) has already made arrangements for comparative coverage from another source.
3. You can find out more about your institutions health insurance policy from their website or your admission package.

SARAH & TOM (Example)

Sarah and Tom (twins) just graduated from High-School and are going to University in September. Sarah is enrolled in a local University within walking distance from her parents' home and is near a bus route. Tom on the other hand is going to a University out of town.

Let's see how other costs can quickly add up. For simplicity, we assume they are taking identical science programs and their tuition fees are identical.

The table below shows how Tom can easily add thousands of dollars to his expenses each year and how he could end up owing a lot more than Sarah at the end of their 4 year university program (*Note: Tuition amounts are excluded from the calculation*).

I am not giving a blanket order for students to go to schools close to home. I however want to show that it is an option worth considering especially when one finds it challenging to finance their education.

Cost Item for 1 Year	Sarah	Tom
Travel (Holidays and Christmas)	$ 0	$500
Furniture	$ 0	$ 200
Rent	$ 0	$ 8000
Groceries	$ 300	$ 3000
Household Supplies	$ 0	$ 100
Laundry & Dry Cleaning	$ 0	$ 416
Cable TV / Internet	$ 0	$ 600
Transportation (bus pass)	$ 480	$ 480
1 Year Total	$ 780	$ 12,756
4 Year Total	$ 3,120	$ 51,564

Lessons Learned From the Twins

By staying at home while going to University, Sarah saves approximately $12,000 a year, which works out to $48,000 for a 4 year program. Tom on the other hand has incurred those additional costs and will have to pay back the amount plus interest after he graduates.

Tom's debt could be a strain on his finances when he moves out on his own and has to make debt repayments in addition to paying his regular living expenses. On a related note, Tom could have used the extra expense incurred while schooling away from home as a future down payment for a house or car.

The main point from this example is you can save a significant amount of money by staying home while going to school. It is definitely an option worth considering when deciding on which post-secondary institution to attend.

CHECKLIST

I included the checklist below to help you stay on track when looking for areas to save money.

You can use it to check-off each area you have examined or completed. Enter your current cost in the "Before Analysis" section and when you make changes, enter your new cost in the "After Analysis" section.

Remember to calculate your "Total Saved" after analysis to see how much you reduce your costs by implementing ideas from this book.

Student Savings Checklist		
Expense Area	Before Analysis	After Analysis
Create Budget		
Accommodation		
Fun		
Food		
Transportation		
Communication		
Books		
Entertainment		
Employment		
Banking		
Credit Card		
Student Discounts		
Total Cost of Ownership		
Scholarships		
Student Loans		
Health & Dental		
Seek Help		
Total		
	Total Saved	

Suggestions

1. Create a comprehensive budget for all your expenses. You want to avoid any large surprises going forward.
2. Arrange student loans as early as possible.
3. Establish good relationships with your bank. Go in and introduce yourself to the loan specialists.
4. Make graduating with minimal debt a priority.
5. Make simple meals instead of buying fast food.
6. When arranging shared accommodations, pick roommates wisely to ensure compatibility - quiet, tidy, respect your stuff, not eating your food, etc.
7. Make sure part-time work does not negatively impact your grades. Adjust your work hours accordingly.

SEEK HELP

If you find yourself in financial trouble where you cannot pay your bills on time or your spending is out of control, it makes sense to reach out for help before things get completely out of hand.

The earlier you start addressing your financial troubles, the sooner you stop digging yourself further into debt, and start making concrete plans to keep it under control.

There is no shame in seeking professional help when we are in over our heads.

Where and From Whom

A number of people or institutions can help you sort out your financial problems and give you guidance to make better choices in the future. They include:

1. Guidance or Financial Counsellors at your school.
2. You parents.
3. Your Financial Institution (Bank or Credit Union).
4. Online.
5. Library.
6. Book Store.

FINAL WORDS

To get the most from this book, remember to first create a budget so you know how much money is coming in and going out. Your budget makes your cash flow areas visible, so you know where to make changes as required.

As a student, and also in life, treat your finances as an important part of your education. The choices you make now will affect your cash flow during your student years and long after your graduate, so choose wisely.

I suggest you make graduating with the least amount of debt a priority and take steps, as indicated in this book, to find ways to constantly reduce your expenses. I also encourage you to have open discussions with your family, friends and other students to find out what they are doing to reduce their expenses. This way you all learn from each other.

Remember, many of the steps to saving money are simple. For example making your sandwich or coffee instead of buying it, buying in bulk (as long as you can consume the items before they go bad), searching for used books and furniture, are simple but effective choices that will help you reduce your living expenses.

The most important thing that determines how much you will save is your discipline and commitment to putting many of the money-saving ideas into practice each day. Every little bit will help you save money and reduce overall debt.

Thank you for reading this book and going through the steps outlined to help you save money. I hope you found it useful and most importantly, that you put into action the suggestions and advice presented.

Feel free to visit our website at **www.ejitech.com** for more money saving tips, and to also post ideas, tips and suggestions from your experience. They make all of us wiser and smarter.

I wish you all the best in your Post-Secondary Education and also in your career after you graduate.

If you enjoyed this book, please take a moment to leave me a review at your favorite retailer.

Thank you.

Emo Ikede.

AUTHOR

Emamoke (Emo) Ikede's passion is teaching people how to quickly become debt free by reducing their monthly expenses. By reputation, he is frequently invited to speak to various business, community and school groups on this topic.

In 2014, he started the **"MoneyWorld"** conference as collaboration between industry experts to teach people how to manage their money. He is an MBA graduate, founder of **EjiTech Group**, and author of a 'How to Save Money' blog (**www.ejitech.com/howtosavemoney**).

He enjoys spending time with his lovely wife and daughter and looks forward to family vacations and road trips.

You can contact him at **www.ejitech.com**